THE RISE OF ENVIRONMENTALISM

AMERICAN ERAS: DEFINING MOMENTS

T0027030

MARTIN GITLIN

CHERRY LAKE PRESS

Published in the United States of America by Cherry Lake Publishing Group
Ann Arbor, Michigan
www.cherrylakepublishing.com

Content Adviser: Kevin Whinnery, MA, History
Reading Adviser: Beth Walker Gambro, MS, Ed., Reading Consultant, Yorkville, IL
Photo Credits: © PA Images / Alamy Stock Photo, cover, 1; © Only_NewPhoto/Shutterstock, 5;
  © University of Michigan School of Environment and Sustainability/Flickr, 7; © Photo by Bill Shrout/
  National Archives Catalog/NA Identifier: 546310, 8; © Boston Public Library/Picryl, 9; © U.S. Fish
  and Wildlife Service Headquarters/flickr, 10; © Photo by Leffler, Warren K./Library of Congress/
  LOC Control No. 2019630903, 13; ©fotografixx/istock, 15; © ChameleonsEye/Shutterstock, 16;
  © Russ Heinl/Shutterstock, 19; © General Design Liquidator/Shutterstock, 20; © MGO/AP Photo, 21;
  © Photo by Marion S. Trikosko/Library of Congress/LOC Control No. 2005696449, 22; © George
  Sheldon/Shutterstock, 25; © George Sheldon/Shutterstock, 26; © Stor24/Shutterstock, 28

Cherry Lake Press is an imprint of Cherry Lake Publishing Group.

Library of Congress Cataloging-in-Publication Data
Names: Gitlin, Marty, author.
Title: The rise of environmentalism / by Martin Gitlin.
Description: Ann Arbor, Michigan : Cherry Lake Publishing Group, [2022] | Series: American eras:
  defining moments | Includes index.
Identifiers: LCCN 2021007829 (print) | LCCN 2021007830 (ebook) | ISBN 9781534187412 (Hardcover) |
  ISBN 9781534188815 (Paperback) | ISBN 9781534190214 (PDF) | ISBN 9781534191617 (ebook)
Subjects: LCSH: Environmentalism—Juvenile literature. | Green movement—Juvenile literature.
Classification: LCC GE195.5 .G535 2021 (print) | LCC GE195.5 (ebook) | DDC 304.20973/09047—dc23
LC record available at https://lccn.loc.gov/2021007829
LC ebook record available at https://lccn.loc.gov/2021007830

Cherry Lake Publishing Group would like to acknowledge the work of the Partnership for 21st Century
Learning, a Network of Battelle for Kids. Please visit http://www.battelleforkids.org/networks/p21
for more information.

Printed in the United States of America
Corporate Graphics

ABOUT THE AUTHOR

Martin Gitlin has written more than 150 educational books. He also won more than 45 awards
during his 11-year career as a newspaper journalist. Gitlin lives in Cleveland, Ohio.

TABLE OF CONTENTS

INTRODUCTION

The date was January 28, 1969. A ship off the coast of California spilled 3 million gallons (11.4 million liters) of oil into the ocean. Thousands of birds, fish, and sea **mammals** were dead.

People in Cleveland, Ohio, witnessed a shocking and disturbing scene 5 months later. The Cuyahoga River was on fire. Local industries had dumped so much oil and chemicals into the waterway that it ignited.

Other distressing news began to filter in that year. The bald eagle, a U.S. national symbol, was becoming extinct due to **pollution**. The eagles were eating fish contaminated by DDT. DDT was a popular chemical used as a **pesticide** on farms. The chemical negatively affected the eagles' ability to properly reproduce.

Such events raised awareness among Americans about the environment. Americans started to understand that they needed to take better care of the water, air, and land. It became more apparent as the 1970s progressed that Earth was in trouble.

The National Environmental Policy Act was signed the very first day of 1970. The Act created a special council that would advise the president on environmental issues.

The United States faced many problems during this period. The Watergate scandal forced President Richard Nixon out of office. An oil shortage sent gas prices soaring. Angry students in Iran took 52 American hostages in 1979.

But only one crisis threatened the very existence of humans on Earth. And that was the one that was destroying the environment. Millions of people knew they had to do something to save the planet, and they began to act during the first year of the 1970s.

CHAPTER 1

Earth Day

One American who had become alarmed about the environment was Gaylord Nelson. The Wisconsin senator decided to take a stand. He worked for 18 tireless years to make a positive impact on the environment. Inspired by the Vietnam War protesters and "**teach-ins**," Senator Nelson organized an event on April 22, 1970. The event was Earth Day.

The plan gained national attention. Americans from across the nation rallied and marched for a healthier planet. Nelson organized Earth Day to teach people around the world about environmental issues. It was supported by people throughout the United States.

The term "Earth Day" was first used by John McConnell. He had organized the first local Earth Day on March 21, 1970.

Young people were especially enthusiastic. More than 10,000 elementary and high schools participated. Over 2,000 colleges joined the cause. Even local communities nationwide were recognizing Earth Day. Overall, about 20 million Americans were involved in the nation's first Earth Day. It was a celebration of and an educational event about the planet on which they lived.

The first Earth Day helped create the EPA and pass laws like the Clean Water, Clean Air, and Endangered Species Acts.

April 22 was chosen to attract and appeal to more college students.
This date fell in between most colleges' spring break and final exams.

American political leaders started to understand the importance of environmental issues. The result was **legislation** that served to clean the water, air, and land. Senator Nelson's plan even led to the establishment of the U.S. Environmental Protection Agency (EPA) on July 9, 1970. The EPA today still serves to protect people and the environment.

Many believe that the 1962 book *Silent Spring* by Rachel Carson helped start the modern environmental movement. The book is about the harmful effects of pesticides.

Earth Day became an annual national event. The event even gained popularity around the world. By 1990, Earth Day went global. America was joined by 141 countries around the world in celebration of Earth. Over 200 million people participated! Today, that number has exploded and grown to about 1 billion people participating in over 190 countries worldwide.

Impactful Ads

In 1975, the EPA came out with a television ad, or public service announcement (PSA), encouraging adults to use public transportation. Think of ads and commercials you've seen. Have any prompted you to take action? What was it about the ad or commercial that made you feel this way? Discuss your thoughts with a family member or friend.

CHAPTER 2

An Environmental Watchdog

Evidence was piling up in the late 1960s that the United States was ruining its environment. The nation required new laws that would safeguard its air, water, and land.

The result was the National Environmental Policy Act (NEPA). It was passed by Congress in 1969 and signed by President Nixon on January 1, 1970. The law established U.S. environmental policy for the future.

NEPA protects local communities from **federal** projects deemed dangerous to the environment or public health. It requires the government to study the projects' impacts to learn of possible harmful effects.

Inspired by NEPA, many other countries and organizations, including Austria, India, and Israel, have created their own environmental impact assessments.

The law recognizes that projects that damage the environment can also be harmful to people. A NEPA review process could discover long-term health risks to the people of a community. Such a project would then be banned until safety changes were made. Only when it is deemed safe can the government follow through with a project.

One example is Plum Island Animal Disease Center in New York. This lab handles extremely dangerous and deadly animal diseases. The federal government wanted to expand this research lab. However, the expansion would have threatened public safety. The small research facility is only 8 miles (13 kilometers) from the Connecticut coast and less than 100 miles (161 km) from New York City, where more than 8 million people live. NEPA was able to challenge this expansion due to security risks, environmental impact, and public safety. The lab moved to a more remote place in Kansas, far from major cities. This addressed the major concerns and allowed the federal government to expand the research facility. The $1.25-billion lab is scheduled to open in 2022 or 2023.

NEPA serves to protect both people and the environment they live in.

Laws like the Clean Air and Clean Water Acts have helped significantly reduce pollution.

A greater understanding of environmental needs led to new legislation in the early 1970s. These laws included the Clean Air Act and the Clean Water Act. The acts targeted businesses such as factories that were releasing dangerous chemicals and waste into the environment.

[21ST CENTURY SKILLS LIBRARY]

The result was a battle between **corporate** America and the health of the water, air, and land. The 1969 incident of the Cuyahoga River catching on fire in Ohio became a symbol of environmental neglect. The river caught on fire at least 13 times before the tragic 1969 event due to industrial waste being dumped into the water.

Greenpeace

One group of **activists** took an aggressive approach to environmental concerns in the 1970s. Greenpeace targeted the whaling industry in one dramatic event in 1975. Its activists sailed on a tiny ship to confront ships of whale hunters. The activists sped their boat between the whaling ships and the whales. The sailors fired a **harpoon** at the activists. But the whaling ship eventually retreated. They didn't want to risk killing humans and creating an international incident. Greenpeace had saved the whales. Were the tactics of Greenpeace too aggressive or justified? Use research to support your argument. Discuss your thoughts and findings with a family member or friend.

CHAPTER 3

The Love Canal

There wasn't much love in the Love Canal in the late 1970s. The Hooker Chemical Company made sure of that when it began using it as a **toxic** waste dump from 1942 to 1953.

Love Canal was located 4 miles (6.4 km) south of Niagara Falls in New York. It was also the name of a nearby community of 800 homes.

Love Canal is in close proximity to Niagara Falls. This made the area appealing to many companies for its hydroelectric power.

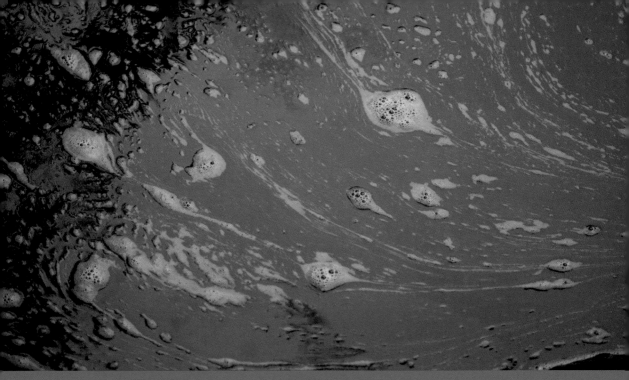

The Love Canal site was used as a toxic chemical waste dump since as early as the 1940s.

Newspaper reports in the late 1970s revealed disturbing trends. People living near the canal were becoming sick. Residents were suffering from illnesses including **epilepsy**, **asthma**, and severe headaches. Babies born in the area also had a high rate of birth defects. The reason? The Hooker Chemical Company had been dumping 21,000 tons of toxic chemicals into the canal.

Communities and neighbors banded together to quickly address the Love Canal problem when they felt public officials weren't taking action.

On August 7, 1978, President Jimmy Carter declared the Love Canal a disaster area.

The chemicals eventually spilled into the basements and yards of neighborhood homes. They infected the playground at a nearby elementary school.

State officials dismissed the citizens' concerns. But President Jimmy Carter declared a state of emergency for the area. He had 239 local families relocated. However, 700 families still remained near the site. They were considered safe and forced to stay. It wasn't until 1981 that President Carter had them moved as well.

Love Canal came to represent environmental tragedies caused by toxic dumps throughout the United States. But good did come out of the Love Canal tragedy. The government passed the Comprehensive Environmental Response, Compensation, and Liability Act (CERLA), in 1980. This act is known as the Superfund law. It provides **resources** including money, cleanup assistance, and emergency response for tragic events like the Love Canal disaster.

The Love Canal incident wasn't the only environmental disaster. Another event around the same time threatened even greater loss of life.

CHAPTER 4

Three Mile Island

It was March 28, 1979. Most of the residents of Middletown, Pennsylvania, were asleep. After all, it was 4:00 a.m.

But they were at risk. A **reactor** at the nearby Three Mile Island **nuclear** power plant was in danger of a disastrous **meltdown**. It threatened to release dangerous **radiation** into the atmosphere. All children and pregnant women living within a 5-mile (8 km) radius were safely evacuated that same day.

Atomic power is used to produce not just weapons, like the atomic bomb, but also power, like nuclear power.

The near-total disaster at Three Mile Island was due to a combination of design flaws, mechanical failure, and human error.

Fortunately, only a small amount of radiation was released. There were no negative health effects on plant workers or the public. But the Three Mile Island nuclear accident was one of the worst in U.S. history. It cost over $1 billion to clean up and fix over the span of 14 years. Studies were performed to determine what went wrong. The goal was to prevent any other meltdowns in the future.

The event quickly changed the nuclear industry. Many planned construction projects on new nuclear plants were canceled. There was a growing anti-nuclear sentiment among people. Many were protesting the use of nuclear power because they were afraid of the risks those nuclear plants posed. These feelings and protests continued from the 1970s to well into the late 1990s and early 2000s.

However, there was good that came from the unfortunate incident. The industry made proactive and positive changes that reduced risks to public safety. Among these changes included emergency response planning, protection against radiation, and reactor training.

The Start of Recycling

The environmental movement of the 1970s played a major role in the push for **recycling**. Previous efforts such as during World War II focused on reusing discarded items for the war effort. But the motivation behind recycling in the 1970s was to limit waste and stop the need for harmful landfills. Oregon became the first state to recycle beverage containers in 1972. Woodbury, New Jersey, was the first community to launch a curbside recycling program in 1980. Think of some other ways besides recycling that limit the amount of trash you throw away. Get creative! Brainstorm with a family member or friend.

There are many ways people and organizations help protect the environment.

Research & Act

People of all ages can start campaigns to help the environment. You and your friends or classmates can contribute in many ways. Among them are drives to gather recyclable items such as rubber, plastic, and paper. For instance, rubber soles can be turned into playground surfaces. Outgrown shoes can be worn again by children in other countries. Research what you can do in your community to improve the environment. Ask for advice from your teacher or parents. Gather friends or classmates and get started!

Timeline

▶ April 22, 1970: **The United States celebrates its first Earth Day.**

▶ December 31, 1970: **President Nixon signs the Clean Air Act into law.**

▶ 1970: **U.S. whaling ends as whales are placed on the endangered species list.**

▶ February 26, 1972: **The Buffalo Creek disaster in West Virginia calls attention to the dangers of strip mining for coal.**

▶ December 16, 1974: **The Safe Drinking Water Act goes into effect.**

▶ April 27, 1975: **Greenpeace activists head out to stop whaling in the Pacific Ocean, marking the beginning of the end for commercial whaling.**

▶ 1977: **Congress passes the Soil and Conservation Act.**

▶ 1978: **Toxic dump disaster overwhelms Love Canal community in New York state.**

▶ March 28, 1979: **The Three Mile Island nuclear plant partially melts down.**

Further Research

BOOKS

Bell, Lucy. *You Can Change the World: The Kids' Guide to a Better Planet.* Kansas City, MO: Andrews McMeel Publishing, 2020.

Knutson, Julie. *Three Mile Island.* Ann Arbor, MI: Cherry Lake Publishing, 2021.

WEBSITES

Ducksters: The Environment
https://www.ducksters.com/science/environment

Greenpeace: Waste-free fun! Games and activities that teach environmental stewardship
https://www.greenpeace.org/static/planet4-international-stateless/2020/05/14bf6e03-pff_games_6-12.pdf

National Geographic Kids: Save the Earth
https://kids.nationalgeographic.com/explore/nature/save-the-earth-hub

Glossary

activists (AK-tih-vists) people working toward social or political change

asthma (AZ-muh) physical condition that limits the ability to breathe

corporate (KOR-puh-ruht) related to a company that legally has the rights and liabilities of an individual

epilepsy (EH-puh-lep-see) a brain disorder that can cause loss of consciousness or seizures

federal (FEH-duh-ruhl) related to the national government

harpoon (har-POON) a sharp spear used to hunt animals such as whales

legislation (leh-juh-SLAY-shuhn) law or set of laws made by a government

mammals (MAH-muhls) animals that feed milk to their young and usually have hair covering much of their bodies

meltdown (MELT-doun) an accident in a nuclear reactor that happens when the fuel overheats and melts the surrounding core and equipment

nuclear (NOO-klee-uhr) relating to energy created when atoms are split apart or joined together

pesticide (PES-tih-side) a chemical used to kill insects or weeds that damage plants or crops

pollution (puh-LOO-shuhn) harmful materials that damage the land, water, or air

radiation (ray-dee-AY-shuhn) energy sent out in the form of rays or particles

reactor (ree-AK-tuhr) large device that produces nuclear energy

recycling (ree-SY-kling) creating something new from something used

resources (REE-sohr-sez) things that are valuable or useful to people

teach-ins (TEECH-inz) meetings usually held on college campuses for people to talk and learn about something

toxic (TAHK-sik) something that is poisonous

INDEX